Boxes of Bags

by Aiden Brown
illustrated by Nelson Jones

Practice Pre-Decodable 14

McGraw Hill Education

Bothell, WA • Chicago, IL • Columbus, OH • New York, NY

MHEonline.com

Send all inquiries to:
McGraw-Hill Education
8787 Orion Place
Columbus, OH 43240

ISBN: 978-0-02-141260-0
MHID: 0-02-141260-X

Printed in the United States of America.

8 9 10 CTM 23

He had  of  .

boxes apples

We had  of  .

bags apples

He had 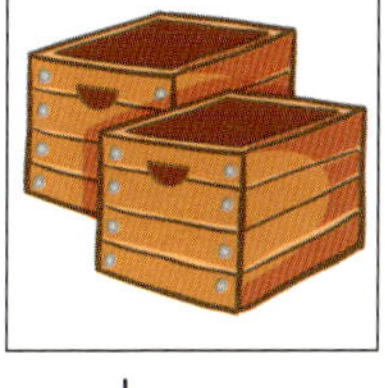 of  .

boxes oranges

We had 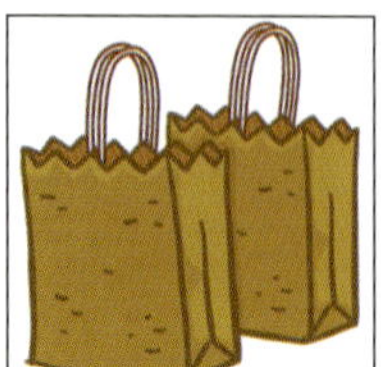 of .

bags

oranges

He had  of  .

boxes corn

We had  of .

boxes bags